BABY GIRAFFES

by Spencer Brinker

Consultant: Beth Gambro
Reading Specialist, Yorkville, Illinois

BEARPORT
PUBLISHING

Minneapolis, Minnesota

Teaching Tips

Before Reading

- Briefly discuss animal life cycles. Babies are born, they grow, and they have their own babies.

- Look through the glossary together. Read and discuss the words.

- Go on a picture walk, looking through the pictures to discuss vocabulary and make predictions about the text.

During Reading

- Encourage readers to point to each word as it is read. Stop occasionally to ask readers to point to a specific word in the text.

- If a reader encounters an unknown word, ask them to look at the rest of the page. Are there any clues to help them understand?

After Reading

- Check for understanding.

  ‣ What are some things baby giraffes do during the first few weeks? What about after that?
  ‣ Find a place in the book that tells you what a baby giraffe looks like.
  ‣ Look at page 22. What did you learn about baby giraffes from reading this book.

- Ask the readers to think deeper.

  ‣ Other than size, what is one thing that is different about baby giraffes and adult giraffes?
  ‣ What is one thing that is similar about baby and adult giraffes?

Credits:

Cover, © Steve and Bryce Kroencke/iStock; 3, © DaddyBit/iStock; 5, © Janugio/iStock; 6-7, © Janugio/iStock; 8, © J. NATAYO/Shutterstock; 9, © Lori Ellis/Shutterstock; 10-11, © Judy Kennamer/Shutterstock; 13, © Janugio/iStock; 14, © Mees Kuiper/Shutterstock; 15, © Faer Out/Shutterstock; 16-17, © DSLR Shooter/Shutterstock; 18-19, © MyImages - Micha/Shutterstock; 21, © PLANET EARTH/Shutterstock; 22, © DaddyBit/iStock; 23TL, © Edwin Butter/Shutterstock; 23TR, © Volodymyr Burdiak/Shutterstock; 23BL, © Janugio/iStock; and 23BR, © leezsnow/iStock.

Library of Congress Cataloging-in-Publication Data

Names: Brinker, Spencer, author.
Title: Baby giraffes / by Spencer Brinker.
Description: Bearcub books. | Minneapolis, Minnesota : Bearport Publishing
  Company, [2021] | Series: Animal babies | Includes bibliographical
  references and index.
Identifiers: LCCN 2020008725 (print) | LCCN 2020008726 (ebook) | ISBN
  9781642809565 (library binding) | ISBN 9781642809633 (paperback) | ISBN
  9781642809701 (ebook)
Subjects: LCSH: Giraffe—Infancy—Juvenile literature.
Classification: LCC QL737.U56 B75 2021 (print) | LCC QL737.U56 (ebook) |
  DDC 599.63813/92—dc23
LC record available at https://lccn.loc.gov/2020008725
LC ebook record available at https://lccn.loc.gov/2020008726

For more information, write to Bearport Publishing, 5357 Penn Avenue South, Minneapolis, MN 55419.

Printed in the United States of America.

Contents

It's a Baby Giraffe!

Plop!

Something drops from a mother giraffe.

It is her baby.

A **calf** falls more than 5 feet (1.5 m) when it is born!

The fall does not hurt the baby giraffe.

The mother begins to lick the calf right away.

Soon, the calf stands up.

The **newborn** is already tall.
It is about as tall as an adult man.

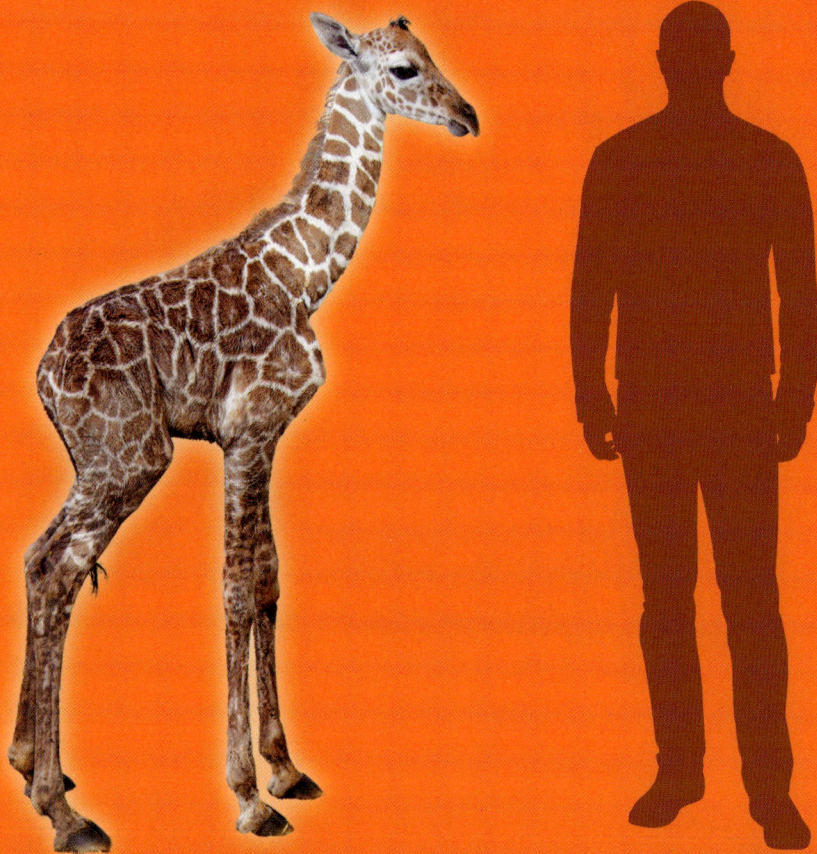

The calf takes its first steps.
Be careful!

The calf is hungry!

It reaches out its long neck.

It drinks milk from its mother's body.

The calf has two **horns** on its head.

Now, the horns lie flat.

When the giraffe is older, the horns will stand up.

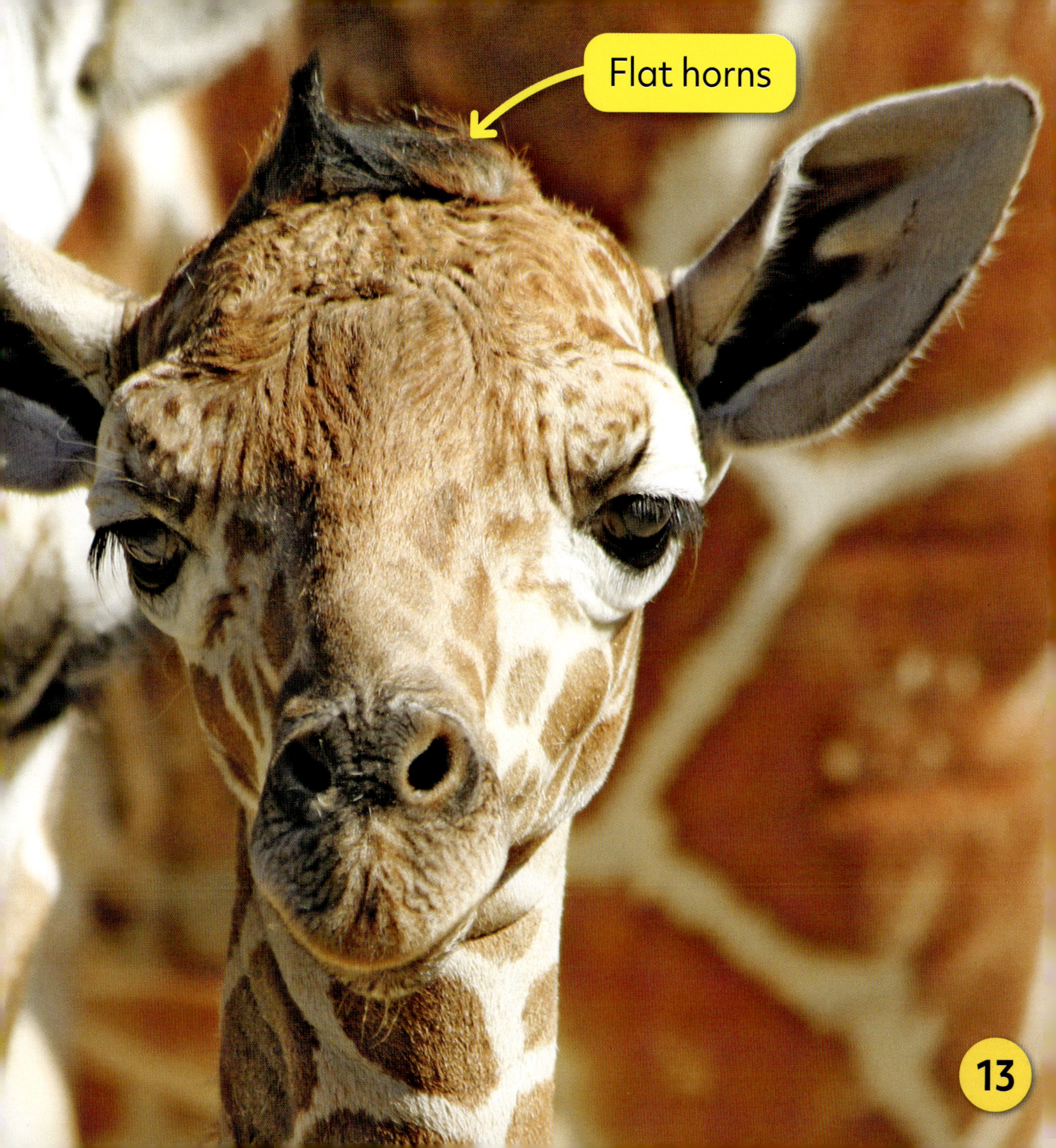
Flat horns

Later that day, the calf can run.

It stays close to its mother and other giraffes.

A group of giraffes
is called a tower.

For the first few weeks, the calf rests a lot.

It lies in the grass.

The spots on its skin help it hide.

A calf drinks milk for about four months.

After that, it eats some leaves, too.

The calf's long **tongue** grabs the new food.

A giraffe is an adult when it is about 4 years old.

Soon it is ready to have its own baby!

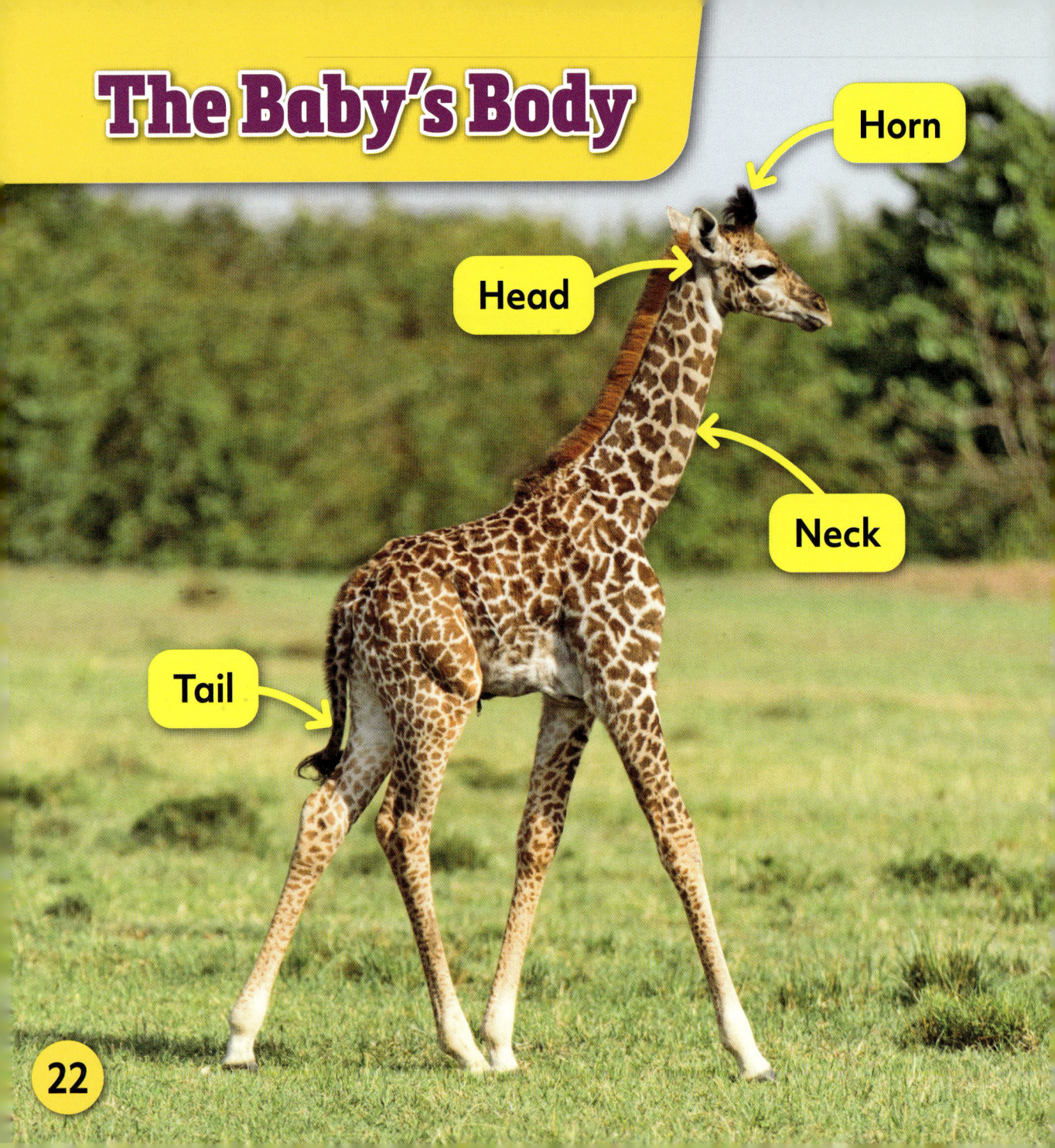

The Baby's Body

Horn

Head

Neck

Tail

Glossary

calf a baby giraffe

horns the hard, bony growths on an animal's head

newborn a baby that was just born

tongue a part of the mouth that tastes and is used in eating

Index

Read More

Borgert–Spaniol, Megan. *Baby Giraffes (Blastoff! Readers. Super Cute!).* Minneapolis: Bellwether Media (2016).

Murray, Julie. *Giraffe Calves (Abdo Kids. Baby Animals).* Minneapolis: Abdo Kids Junior (2019).

Learn More Online

1. Go to **www.factsurfer.com**
2. Enter "**Baby Giraffes**" into the search box.
3. Click on the cover of this book to see a list of websites.

About the Author

Spencer Brinker loves to tell "dad jokes" and play word games with his twin girls.